Real-World STEM:
Reverse Engineer
the Brain

Other titles in the *Real-World STEM* series include:

Real-World STEM: Reverse Engineer the Brain

Christine Wilcox

ReferencePoint
Press®

San Diego, CA

© 2018 ReferencePoint Press, Inc.
Printed in the United States

For more information, contact:
ReferencePoint Press, Inc.
PO Box 27779
San Diego, CA 92198
www.ReferencePointPress.com

LIBRARY OF CONGRESS CATALOGING-IN-PUBLICATION DATA

Name: Wilcox, Christine
Title: Real-World STEM: Reverse Engineer the Brain/by Christine Wilcox.
Description: San Diego, CA: ReferencePoint Press, Inc., 2018. | Series:
Real-World STEM | Audience: Grade 9 to 12. | Includes bibliographical
    references and index.
Identifiers: LCCN 2017023861 (print) | ISBN
    9781682822470 (hardback) | ISBN 9781682822487 (eBook)

CONTENTS

Great Engineering Achievements

1

Electrification
Vast networks of electricity provide power for the developed world.

2

Automobile
Revolutionary manufacturing practices made cars more reliable and affordable, and the automobile became the world's major mode of transportation.

3

Airplane
Flying made the world accessible, spurring globalization on a grand scale.

4

Water Supply and Distribution
Engineered systems prevent the spread of disease, increasing life expectancy.

5

Electronics
First with vacuum tubes and later with transistors, electronic circuits underlie nearly all modern technologies.

6

Radio and Television
These two devices dramatically changed the way the world receives information and entertainment.

7

Agricultural Mechanization
Numerous agricultural innovations led to a vastly larger, safer, and less costly food supply.

8

Computers
Computers are now at the heart of countless operations and systems that impact people's lives.

9

Telephone
The telephone changed the way the world communicates personally and in business.

10

Air Conditioning and Refrigeration
Beyond providing convenience, these innovations extend the shelf life of food and medicines, protect electronics, and play an important role in health care delivery.

11 Highways

Forty-four thousand miles of US highways enable personal travel and the wide distribution of goods.

12 Spacecraft

Going to outer space vastly expanded humanity's horizons and resulted in the development of more than sixty thousand new products on Earth.

Internet

The Internet provides a global information and communications system of unparalleled access.

13

14 Imaging

Numerous imaging tools and technologies have revolutionized medical diagnostics.

15 Household Appliances

These devices have eliminated many strenuous and laborious tasks.

16 Health Technologies

From artificial implants to the mass production of antibiotics, these technologies have led to vast health improvements.

17 Petroleum and Petrochemical Technologies

These technologies provided the fuel that energized the twentieth century.

18 Laser and Fiber Optics

Their applications are wide and varied, including almost simultaneous worldwide communications, noninvasive surgery, and point-of-sale scanners.

19 Nuclear Technologies

From splitting the atom came a new source of electric power.

20 High-Performance Materials

They are lighter, stronger, and more adaptable than ever before.

Source: Wm. A. Wulf, "Great Achievements and Grand Challenges," National Academy of Engineering, *The Bridge*, Fall/Winter 2000. www.nae.edu.

INTRODUCTION

Is the Brain a Supercomputer?

"No matter how hard they try, brain scientists and cognitive psychologists will never find a copy of Beethoven's 5th Symphony in the brain—or copies of words, pictures, grammatical rules or any other kinds of environmental stimuli. The human brain . . . does not contain most of the things people think it does—not even simple things such as 'memories.' . . . Given this reality, why do so many scientists talk about our mental life as if we were computers?"

—Robert Epstein, senior research psychologist

Robert Epstein, "The Empty Brain," *Aeon*, May 18, 2016. https://aeon.co.

The human brain is the most complicated structure in the universe. It is made up of a staggeringly intricate web of connections—billions of cells (called neurons) that reach out to each other with threadlike arms, strengthening and weakening their bonds, coupling and uncoupling at trillions of junctures. Electrical impulses that travel along these bonds release a cascading wave of chemical messages that direct everything from movement to bodily functions to emotional states. But thought—from which intelligence arises—seems to be generated somehow by the electrical impulses themselves, which change the state of the neurons through which they travel. To employ a metaphor, if these neurons were a vast orchestra, then thought would be the infinite number of harmonies they can create together—harmonies that are not made of matter but exist just the same.

The brain-as-orchestra metaphor does not really explain intelligence. After all, instruments, sound waves, and music have little to do with neurons, electrical impulses, and thought. But when an idea is complex and difficult to grasp, people try to understand it by comparing it to a more familiar concept.

Throughout history, dozens of metaphors have been used to help people understand the brain. The most recent one is brain-as-computer—an especially apt metaphor because computers were created to take over intellectual tasks that are particularly difficult for people. Computers excel at performing calculations, finding patterns in vast amounts of data, and making decisions based on logic and mathematical probability. They are the ultimate information processors.

Understanding the Inner Workings of the Brain ■

However, as soon as the computer became a metaphor for the brain, members of the scientific community made what psychologist Robert Epstein sees as a crucial mistake. They assumed that, because these artificial information processors could mimic intelligent behavior, then everything that is capable of intelligence must therefore be an information processor. In other words, the metaphor of brain-as-computer was no longer just a metaphor. As Epstein explains, "For more than half a century now, psychologists, linguists, neuroscientists and other experts on human behavior have been asserting that the human brain works like a computer."[1]

This idea guided research into artificial intelligence (AI) for most of the second half of the twentieth century. The actual inner workings of the brain were ignored by most AI scientists, who tried to make computers smarter by improving their information-processing abilities. But finding patterns and performing calculations is just one small facet of intelligence. Early versions of AI could not learn, generalize, or solve problems that any three-year-old child could solve, like recognizing faces or understanding simple concepts. Research efforts stalled, and while computers got faster and more powerful, they did not get much smarter. And scientists were no closer to understanding what, exactly, intelligence is.

It eventually became clear that if scientists wanted to create AI, they had to understand how the brain works. AI researchers began

WORDS IN CONTEXT

neuron

a brain cell or nerve cell that transmits signals to the brain or body, these signals control the body and are responsible for thought

to reverse engineer the structure and behavior of neurons, creating new technologies that allowed computers to learn through a process of observation and trial and error. This revolutionary technique is called machine learning, and it has given computers the ability to do many things that only humans could do in the past, such as play rule-based games and use language.

The success of machine learning led to an explosion of research in AI and reverse engineering the brain. In the early 2000s some of the world's biggest technology companies, such as Google and IBM, poured billions into new AI research divisions. Data-rich companies like Amazon and Facebook jumped on the bandwagon as well, refining AI technologies and using them to expand their businesses. Today whole industries are banking that AI will revolutionize society, and they are pouring resources into developing new ways to understand how the brain works and create intelligence through computer technology.

Creating Human-Level Intelligence ■

The holy grail of AI research is to create AI that has human-level intelligence. This, experts believe, will not be possible until 2030 at the earliest. The challenges researchers face are monumental. The human brain has yet to be mapped; in fact, scientists are still struggling to map neurons in the brains of mice. And they are no further along in understanding what, exactly, intelligence is and how it emerges in a biological system. In addition, even though computers and brains do not work in the same way, computers are still the best technology we have to create AI. The biological function of the brain not only has to be understood, it must be re-created in artificial form and made to follow computational principals.

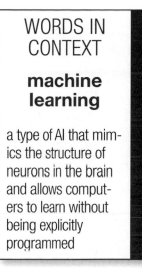

WORDS IN CONTEXT

machine learning

a type of AI that mimics the structure of neurons in the brain and allows computers to learn without being explicitly programmed

Most AI scientists still believe that the brain is a type of supercomputer—in the sense that it is an information processor and its inner workings can be represented by mathematical formulas. According to Gary Marcus, professor of psychology and neural science at New York University, "[Brains] are just exceptionally complex arrangements of matter. . . . There is no reason to think that brains are exempt from the laws of computation. If the heart is a biological pump, and the nose is a biological filter, the brain is a biological computer, a machine for processing information in lawful, systematic ways."[2] The trick, most AI researchers believe, is to uncover the laws that underlie the brain's structure and then re-create them in digital form.

Whether researchers will succeed in developing computers that have human-level intelligence is still unknown. But nearly all AI experts agree that the best chance humanity has in meeting this grand challenge is to reverse engineer the brain.

CHAPTER 1

CURRENT STATUS:
The Golden Age of Artificial Intelligence

"The dream is finally arriving. This is what it was all leading up to. We've made more progress in the last five years than at any time in history."

—Bill Gates, cofounder of Microsoft

Quoted in Liana Baker, "Tech Moguls Declare Era of Artificial Intelligence," Reuters, June 2, 2016. www.reuters.com.

When most people think of AI, they imagine the human-like robots that are a staple of science fiction. But a robot—whether it is an intelligent android in a movie or a vacuum that runs by itself—is merely the container for AI. AI is the computer (or, more accurately, the computer code) that controls the robot. In fact, most AI in use today does not make use of a robot or other complex interface. For example, when an online video streaming service suggests videos to watch next, it is using AI. This is a fairly unsophisticated form of AI—it is simply an algorithm, or set of instructions, that is designed to make predictions about viewers' likes and dislikes based on their viewing history. But because *artificial intelligence* is defined by *Merriam-Webster* as "the capacity of a machine to imitate intelligent human behavior,"[3] this simple predictive algorithm is indeed AI. Using that definition, AI encompasses everything from a handheld calculator to IBM's question-answering AI, Watson, which beat the reigning *Jeopardy!* champion in 2011. It also includes devices that use AI technologies to restore brain function—for instance, implants that help people see or hear.

The term *artificial intelligence* was coined in 1955 by Stanford researcher John McCarthy during a meeting of computer scientists that is now referred to as the Dartmouth Conference. McCarthy and his colleagues proposed that "every aspect of learning or any other feature of intelligence can in principle be so precisely described that a machine can be made to simulate it."[4] In other words, they wanted to reverse engineer human intelligence and then simulate it using a computer. They suggested seven areas of AI research. These areas have been modified over the years, but in general, AI researchers still seek to create computers that can do the following: perceive their environment, use natural language, learn, form concepts, reason and solve problems, behave creatively, and improve themselves.

In the decades since the Dartmouth Conference, researchers have made great strides in perception, language use, and learning. For instance, computers can now see, hear, and sense things

A woman looks at suggested shows and movies to watch next on her Netflix homepage. Netflix uses an algorithm that makes predictions about a viewer's likes and dislikes based on their viewing history—a basic form of artificial intelligence.

about the environment (known as computer perception); process and converse
in human speech (known as natural language processing, or NLP); and learn autonomously (known as machine learning).
In fact, some of these uses of AI—such as
Google's search engine or computer dic-
tation applications—are so commonplace
that people do not think of them as AI at
all. As Kris Hammond, cofounder of the AI
company Narrative Science, explains, "The
minute we can automate a task, we down-
grade the relevant skill involved to one of
mere mechanism."[5]

Two Types of AI ■

AI can be broken down into two broad categories: artificial general intelligence (AGI) and artificial narrow intelligence (ANI). AGI is
also referred to as strong AI. The goal of AGI is to develop an artificial brain that can apply itself to any problem and reason a solution without being programmed to do so by a human being. AGI
depends heavily on reverse engineering both intelligence and the
physical workings of the brain. While the quest for AGI is the most
exciting field of AI research today, it has not yet been achieved.

ANI, which is sometimes referred to as weak AI or applied AI,
is the AI that is in use today. ANI is limited to a single application or
function. For instance, an ANI system that is designed to recognize
human faces, such as Google Cloud Vision, cannot also play a
game or predict a customer's buying habits. Multiple ANI systems
can be combined to form more useful tools, such as Apple's personal assistant, Siri, which can understand speech, answer simple
questions, and perform computer-based tasks. However, combining various ANI tools does not give rise to AGI. In other words,
even though Siri seems to have general intelligence, it is merely a
collection of ANI expert systems designed to do a variety of tasks.

Strategies to Achieve AI ■

Early AI researchers disagreed about how best to advance AI. Some
believed that the best way to create AGI is to study the human brain
and try to replicate its functioning. Others believed that it was not

14

necessary to replicate the brain to simulate intelligence—especially since computers can do many things faster and more accurately than humans can. Because not much was known about how intelligence emerges in the human brain, most researchers pursued the first strategy. They attempted to write comprehensive computer programs that contain the world's knowledge and rules for logical reasoning. This strategy is often referred to as symbolic AI.

In the first few decades after the Dartmouth Conference, AI researchers created algorithms that worked like if-then decision trees (for example, if X happens, do Y). This method was very labor intensive. For instance, to create a chess-playing algorithm, researchers had to program a computer with the ability to evaluate all potential moves on the board in light of the rules and strategies of the game. In other words, the researchers had to thoroughly understand chess in order to write their algorithms.

One of the first examples of a big ANI system that used this type of symbolic AI was IBM's Deep Blue, a chess-playing computer. In 1996 Deep Blue beat Garry Kasparov, who was then the reigning world champion at chess. Deep Blue was successful

In 1996, Garry Kasparov, the reigning world champion of chess, was defeated by IBM's chess-playing computer Deep Blue. Deep Blue was successful because it could evaluate 200 million chess positions per second.

because it was so powerful; it was able to evaluate 200 million chess positions per second, and it could process millions of potential moves and their consequences before moving a chess piece. Even though people use an entirely different method of analysis to play a complex and strategic game such as chess, Deep Blue was able to leverage its computational power (which was massive for its time) to beat a person.

There are significant limitations to ANI systems like Deep Blue. First of all, their programing is labor intensive—programmers have to manually translate knowledge and skills into computer-friendly data and algorithms. Second, this approach works well only when the rules and parameters are clear—such as in mathematics or

The Turing Test

The Turing test was developed in 1950 by Alan Turing, an English mathematician and computer scientist who is widely credited with being the father of AI. Turing's test determines if a machine has the ability to exhibit intelligent behavior. In the standard version of the test, the examiner converses (by exchanging written messages) with both humans and AIs and must determine which of its conversation partners is a machine. The test does not measure true intelligence; rather, it tests a computer's ability to simulate intelligent behavior. This, Turing thought, was at least an answerable question, since there is no agreement among scientists as to what intelligence is and how to define it.

AI scientists do not use the Turing test, because it is subjective. There are, however, many Turing test competitions around the world. Critics say these competitions encourage developers to create AI that tries to trick judges. For instance, at a competition held at the Royal Society in London in 2014, an AI called Eugene convinced one-third of the judges it was a thirteen-year-old boy by using humor and changing the subject whenever it did not understand what a judge was saying.

The most influential Turing test competition is the Loebner Prize, which awards a cash prize each year to the most human-like AI in its competition. A grand prize is offered to an AI that can actually convince a panel of judges that it is human. However, this prize has never been won.

a game like chess. As soon as the relationships between data become vague or hard to define, programming simply becomes too complex to be a viable option.

Once the limitations of symbolic AI became apparent, researchers began modeling AI on a structure that more closely resembled the way the human brain worked. As Gideon Lewis-Kraus, a fellow at the think tank New America, explains, researchers revived the idea that "the best model for flexible automated intelligence was the brain itself." Lewis-Kraus says the researchers decided that computers should "learn from the ground up (from data) rather than from the top down (from rules)."[6] This idea ushered in a new avenue of AI research: machine learning.

Machine Learning ■

Machine learning is a field of AI involved in creating computers that can learn on their own. As Bernard Marr, author of *Data Strategy*, explains, "Engineers realized that rather than teaching computers and machines how to do everything, it would be far more efficient to code them to think like human beings, and then plug them into the internet to give them access to all of the information in the world."[7] While the idea of machine learning has been around for decades, it was not until the world's information became readily available—in the form of the Internet—that the technology took off. Machine learning is now widely available to the public and in use by most major businesses today.

Machine learning is a process in which a computer learns by recognizing patterns, making predictions, and self-correcting based on whether its predictions are right or wrong. For instance, imagine a computer is learning how to recognize a cat. The computer is first "trained" by being shown hundreds of thousands of images of cats, which it analyzes, noting the things that are similar and different about the images. Next it is shown images it has never seen before, and it compares them to the store of knowledge it has accumulated about cats. It then refines its knowledge about what a cat looks like by receiving feedback, in the form of labeled data, about its successes and mistakes—a process that is sort of like checking the caption on a photograph to see what it is.

For example, if the computer has learned that a cat has four legs, it may mistake a table for a cat. Making this mistake helps it learn that when four legs are straight and smooth, it is unlikely that they belong to a cat. This is an oversimplification, of course—machine-learning algorithms allow computers to analyze thousands of elements of a single image in a fraction of a second. But the principle is the same: The computer learns through trial and error, increasing its accuracy over time.

Machine learning can also be used to predict the future, which is especially useful in business applications. For instance, when machine-learning techniques are applied to online retail, computers are able to analyze customers' behavior online, make predictions about future behavior, and learn from successes and mistakes. These techniques can be applied to almost any business that has collected large amounts of customer data. For example, the online retailer Amazon offers a machine-learning service to its sellers that it says can "predict how many . . . products will be sold in future fiscal quarters based on a particular demographic; or estimate which customer profile has the highest probability to become dissatisfied or the most loyal to your brand."[8]

Computer Perception ■

Experiments in image recognition were possible because of advancements in another area of AI: computer vision. Computer vision is a type of computer perception, or the ability to take in information through technology that mimics human senses. By using computer-vision technology, computers can analyze the color and shading of individual pixels and the patterns they form.

But for a computer to truly see, it must do more than just analyze pixels. "To take pictures is not the same as to see, and to see, we really mean understanding," explains computer scientist Fei-Fei Li, director of Stanford's Artificial Intelligence Lab and Vision Lab. "Vision begins with the eyes, but it truly takes place in the brain."[9] The brain, in the case of computer-vision systems, is machine-learning technology. By combining machine learning with pixel analysis, computer-vision systems can analyze millions of images on the Internet to define every possible variation of an object. Using this technique, computer-vision AI can learn to recognize patterns and ultimately make meaning.

Computer-vision technology is now in use in many different products. For instance, computer-vision algorithms can recognize objects, scenes, faces, and even expressions of faces in photographs and videos. Google uses this technology to allow users to search for images on the Internet, and social media platforms like Facebook, Instagram, and Pinterest use it to enhance their user experience. Computer vision can also be used to diagnose diseases. For instance, in 2017 researchers at Stanford University created a computer-vision algorithm that could diagnose skin cancer as accurately as a dermatologist. Some computer-vision technologies can even "see" real objects in space. For instance, the popular video game console Wii senses the movements of a human player and translates them into game play. This type of technology is also used in automobile collision warning systems and in self-driving cars.

Computer-perception technologies are not limited to vision—some can analyze and translate sound and touch. Sound technologies are part of the AI within the cochlear implant, a device that translates sound into electrical signals and allows deaf people to hear. Touch perception technologies are used in robot prostheses, which translate sensory input into electronic signals that are picked up by the human nervous system. The AI within cutting edge robot prostheses allows people to feel the sensation of touch through sensors on those artificial limbs.

Natural Language Processing ■

The third area of AI that researchers have made great advances in is NLP. Language is far too complex to be coded with symbolic AI, as early efforts at translation programs illustrated. Early translation programs contained definitions of every word in two languages and the languages' corresponding rules of grammar. However, it was impossible for humans to also program them with the infinite number of variations in meaning that are derived from context, or the meaning of surrounding words in a sentence or paragraph. For instance, as Lewis-Kraus explains, symbolic AI is likely to translate a phrase like "minister of agriculture" as "priest of farming."[10] According to technology consultant Robin Sandhu, "The challenge with machine translation technologies is not in translating words, but in preserving the meaning of sentences, a complex technological issue that is at the heart of NLP."[11]

Machine learning solved this problem for NLP researchers. By exposing NLP algorithms to millions of examples of the relationships between words, these systems were able to predict, with increasing accuracy, the meaning of a particular word based on its context. This more closely mimics the way that young children learn language. As Lewis-Kraus explains, "Humans don't learn to understand language by memorizing dictionaries and grammar books, so why should we possibly expect our computers to do so?"[12]

Once NLP was able to grasp the meaning of words in context, it became enormously useful. NLP, which includes both text-based and speech-based technologies, is now used in hundreds of different applications. For instance, NLP runs the software that allows virtual personal assistants and AI chatbots (programs that converse with humans via text messages) to understand questions and carry on simple conversations. It is behind applications that summarize blocks of text and those that spot plagiarism in student essays. It is used by the financial industry to extract information from news releases and adjust financial trading algorithms accordingly—a useful tool in an industry where responding quickly to news of company mergers or earnings reports can translate into millions of dollars of profit. NLP can even judge sentiment— determining if a block of text is conveying a positive or negative emotion. Sentiment analysis has many applications, including giving companies the ability to scan social media for mentions of their products to judge if they are perceived positively or negatively—a service that is offered by social media apps like Twitter.

In fact, NLP has become so advanced at understanding meaning and sentiment that it can now generate original news stories on what it reads. Major news groups like the Associated Press regularly use NLP software to produce reports and articles about fast-breaking news stories. While robo-journalism, as it is commonly called, has many limitations, studies have found that many readers cannot tell if simple news articles are written by a

Virtual Assistants

One of the most exciting and successful applications of NLP is the voice-controlled virtual assistant. One such assistant is Alexa, the AI that powers Amazon Echo. Echo is a small, speaker-like computer device that can connect wirelessly to the Internet and smart home devices, such as lighting systems, thermostats, and entertainment systems. Alexa interprets voice commands and performs a wide variety of tasks: It can create shopping lists, search the web, shop online through Amazon, play music, and get weather reports.

Amazon is currently updating the NLP in Alexa and improving its ability to understand its users. For instance, Alexa will be able to access more information about users to help determine their likes and dislikes and to better understand their requests. In addition, researchers are working on integrating NLP technology that will be able to perceive emotion in speech (such as impatience, sarcasm, gratitude, and so on).

What Alexa and other virtual assistants cannot yet do is use machine-learning techniques after they are put into use. If they could, they could tailor their services to better anticipate individual consumers' needs and fulfill their requests. Users could also train them to do specific skills. Improvements like these could eventually make virtual assistants much more useful to the average consumer.

human or a machine. And the technology is constantly improving. "A machine will win a Pulitzer one day," predicts Hammond, who believes that robo-journalism, combined with advanced AI, will one day be able "to tell the stories hidden in data"[13] that human journalists might overlook.

Cognitive Computing ■

Advances in machine learning, computer perception, and NLP led to an enormously important leap in AI development. Once computers could extract meaning from text, sound, and images, all the information on the Internet became available to machine-learning systems. The Internet is increasingly becoming the repository of the sum of all human knowledge and experience, and that information is now in a form that computers can consume with ease. This allowed researchers to use machine learning to create AI that could analyze an enormous amount to general knowledge and become expert in a variety of areas at once.

In 2011 IBM unveiled a new type of generalized AI, which it called Watson. Watson is a computer that was created to be a question answerer. Question answering (QA) is an area of AI concerned with developing systems that use machine learning and NLP to answer questions posed by humans. QA is more advanced than the speech or text generated by chatbots, personal assistants, or even robo-journalism programs—all of which use limited data sets and templates to communicate in narrow subject areas. Instead, Watson uses logic and reasoning to answer questions. As Hammond explains, "Watson builds up evidence for the answers it finds by looking at thousands of pieces of text that give it a level of confidence in its conclusion. It combines the ability to recognize patterns in text with the very different ability to weigh the evidence that matching those patterns provides."[14] This ability to weigh evidence was designed to mimic a person's ability to take various factors into account when weighing the probability that an answer is correct—in other words, to make a best guess. "Just like people," Hammond says, "Watson is able to notice patterns in text that provide a little bit of evidence and then add all that evidence up to get to an answer."[15]

In 2011 Watson, which had been preloaded with 200 million pages of information (much of it from the online encyclopedia *Wikipedia*) beat two human contestants on the quiz show *Jeopardy!* The AI that powers Watson, called DeepQA, was modified to play the game, which asks contestants to provide questions to answers. As information technology reporter Jo Best explains:

> First up, DeepQA works out what the question is asking, then works out some possible answers based on the information it has to hand, creating a thread for each. Every thread uses hundreds of algorithms to study the evidence, looking at factors including what the information says, what type of information it is, its reliability, and how likely

it is to be relevant, then creating an individual weighting based on what Watson has previously learned about how likely they are to be right. It then generated a ranked list of answers, with evidence for each of its options.[16]

Watson then needed to provide the highest-ranking answer before its human opponents could, which usually meant completing its analysis in a fraction of a second. While it made several notable errors (including placing the Canadian city Toronto in the United States), it easily beat two of the game's all-time best players.

Watson can be modified and trained for use in a wide variety of applications. Since its win on *Jeopardy!* in 2011, it has been adapted to assist in business, medical research, the work of accountants and lawyers, and even creative work. Its most ambitious project was to assist oncologists in improving cancer care by sifting through the thousands of research papers published every year and offering treatment options. This project, which was

In 2011 a computer developed by IBM called Watson beat two champions on the popular game show Jeopardy!. Watson had been preloaded with 200 million pages of information, much of it from the online source Wikipedia.

launched in 2013 at the MD Anderson Cancer Center at the University of Texas, was abandoned in 2017—but not because Watson was not up to the task. "The problem is not that there is too much information, but rather there is too little . . . only a handful of published articles are high-quality, randomized trials,"[17] explains health economist David Howard. Without a vast data set to learn from, Watson was unable to perform as well as oncologists.

Watson is an example of AI that reasons—an area of AI that researchers must master in order to achieve AGI. However, it still needs large quantities of labeled data to be able to build up a knowledge base from which to reason—a labor-intensive process that must be done by humans. Watson is a prime example of how far machine learning has come—and how much it still needs to advance.

CHAPTER 2

LIMITATIONS:
Why Artificial Intelligence Is Not Smarter—Yet

"Artificial neural networks are still incredibly primitive compared to biological neural networks, and don't learn the way real brains do."

—Xaq Pitkow, neuroscientist

Quoted in Graciela Gutierrez, "Unlocking the Secrets of the Brain's Intelligence to Develop Smarter Technologies," Baylor College of Medicine, March 10, 2016. www.bcm.edu.

In 2016 a game-playing AI called AlphaGo achieved the most significant breakthrough in AI to date. AlphaGo had been trained to play the ancient Chinese board game Go—the most complex game ever created. While the rules and strategy of Go are simple, the game has 10^{360} (a 10 followed by 360 zeros) possible moves. Considering there are about 10^{80} atoms in the entire universe, this number is staggering. For this reason, experts believed it would be five to ten years before a game-playing AI could master Go. Yet AlphaGo was able to teach itself the game and defeat the reigning world champion, the South Korean professional Go player Lee Sedol.

AlphaGo's win over Sedol was significant for several reasons. First, it illustrated the sheer power of machine learning. Second, unlike most ANIs, AlphaGo uses general purpose algorithms that allow it to learn other types of games without significant retooling. Finally, when playing against Sedol, AlphaGo employed unexpected and unique strategies—strategies that suggested that this sophisticated AI was somehow able to employ creativity.

But the successes of AlphaGo brought with them further challenges for AI researchers. For one thing, machine learning is so

powerful and complex that experts cannot explain the reasoning process an AI like AlphaGo uses to reach its conclusions—an issue that researchers refer to as the black box problem. (In computer science, the term *black box* refers to any system that works in a way that its creators cannot see or understand.) Second, like all machine-learning-based AI, AlphaGo overwrites all accumulated knowledge when it learns a new game. This processes is known as catastrophic forgetting (catastrophic, in this usage, means total), and it means that AlphaGo cannot build on what it has learned in the past. Finally, even though AlphaGo employed creativity in its problem solving, its creators do not know how to replicate this new skill.

The limitations of AlphaGo illustrate how far researchers are from developing human-level AI. By examining these limitations, it is possible to get a better sense of the challenges researchers face in their quest to create AGI.

Neural Networks and Brain Plasticity ■

Machine learning is key to AI, but machine learning would not exist without artificial neural networks (ANNs). ANNs were developed by reverse engineering the way the brain uses biological neurons to processes information. To use an analogy, if machine-learning algorithms are the software behind AI, ANNs are the hardware.

An understanding of ANNs requires a basic understanding of how the brain works. The human brain is made up of about 100 billion neurons. These neurons are designed to physically connect together by growing fibrous threads called axons and dendrites. Axons and dendrites branch out and connect to neighboring neurons so that they can pass information—in the form of electrical impulses and chemical signals—from one neuron to the next. Each neuron can have up to 10,000 connections, which means there are between 100 trillion and 1,000 trillion connections within a typical brain.

All of these interconnected neurons form pathways, like intersecting roads in a busy city. But unlike roads in a city, the pathways are always changing. Those that are used more often become stronger and thicker, like superhighways. And those that are rarely used become weaker, eventually being dismantled. This process is known as brain plasticity, a term that means the brain is constantly changing—making new connections, strengthening well-used connections, and eliminating connections that are no longer useful.

Scientists are not sure how this mass of ever-changing neural connections allows people to recall a memory, perform a calculation, or have a conversation. But they do know that when people do such things, electrical impulses travel along the vast

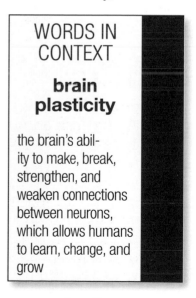

WORDS IN CONTEXT

brain plasticity

the brain's ability to make, break, strengthen, and weaken connections between neurons, which allows humans to learn, change, and grow

number of neural pathways in the brain. These neural pathways connect regions that specialize in different functions, such as emotion, visual processing, memory, and cognitive function. Along the way, these electrical impulses cause neurons to release a cascade of chemicals called neurotransmitters that communicate information from one neuron to the next. Out of this ever-evolving mass of electrical impulses and chemical signals arise thought, imagination, and consciousness. Scientists do not understand how this happens either, but some believe it is a natural process that occurs when a neural network gets complex enough.

Artificial Neural Networks ■

ANNs are designed by using the same general principles found within natural neural networks. ANNs process data within artificial neurons called nodes. These tiny processing units are connected together in a dense, multilayered web. Like those in the brain, the connections between nodes are changeable or "plastic"—they get stronger or weaker depending on whether a connection turns out to be helpful or unhelpful.

The trial-and-error process of machine learning works because of ANNs. As a machine-learning algorithm processes data, the ANN strengthens or weakens its connections, adjusting the probability that a particular pattern of information is important or useful. (Of course, computer nodes are not connected by physical wires that become thicker or thinner. Instead, the strength of connections is based on mathematics and probability.) For example, imagine a computer-vision system is using its ANN to learn to identify a dog. If almost all the dogs it views have tails, the connections between nodes representing "tail" and "dog" become strengthened. Eventually, "tail" becomes an important feature of the AI's concept of "dog."

The type of machine learning performed by very large and complex ANNs like Watson and AlphaGo is referred to as deep learning—the word *deep* refers to the depth of the layers of nodes in the network. Deep learning can produce remarkable results, but the ANN it uses is still much less complex than the human brain. Humans also do not learn by viewing thousands

The Chinese Academy of Sciences introduced its new deep learning processor in 2016. Like AlphaGo and Watson, the Chinese project would have very large artificial neural networks that were much less complex than the human brain but still remarkable for what they could do.

of images and building knowledge from the ground up, pixel by pixel. Rather, people generalize and form concepts, concerning themselves with meaning rather than identification. Because of these differences, even a sophisticated ANN that has learned how to identify a dog still does not know what a dog is; it simply knows that pixels arranged in certain patterns are likely have the label "dog."

The Black Box Problem ■

One problem with ANNs is that there is no way to trace the vast number of connections between nodes in the network. Since ANNs teach themselves, the process they use to reach conclusions is a

Neurotransmitters, Dopamine, and Learning

Neurotransmitters are chemical signaling molecules that neurons produce that control various functions in the body. They do things like accelerate heartbeat; control sleep patterns; and cause feelings of motivation, aversion, or focus. Depending on how they are classified, there are between thirty and one hundred different types of neurotransmitters.

Some brain disorders, such as depression or Parkinson's disease, are caused by too little of a particular neurotransmitter. Doctors attempt to increase levels by prescribing medication that floods the brain with that neurotransmitter. However, scientists have discovered that the release and uptake of neurotransmitters in the brain is an incredibly precise process. Neuroscientist Christof Koch believes that flooding the whole brain with a neurotransmitter is like pouring oil over a car and hoping some drips into the motor.

Neurotransmitters do not create thought, but they do play a crucial role in emotion and learning. Emotions like pleasure, satisfaction, anticipation, and aversion are key to learning. Without these emotions, people would not learn to repeat some experiences and avoid others. The neurotransmitter dopamine causes most of the emotions associated with learning, which in turn helps strengthen memories. In other words, humans learn and remember things because dopamine makes them seem important.

As scientists learn more about how neurotransmitters impact learning, they may be able to use that knowledge to improve machine learning techniques and help AI learn more like humans.

mystery. This is known as the black box problem. As Joel Dudley, director of biomedical informatics at Mount Sinai School of Medicine, explains, "We can build these models, but we don't know how they work."[18]

Scientists have tried several techniques to attempt to reveal how ANNs operate, but they have not been very successful. For instance, in 2015 researchers at Google tackled this problem by running a computer-vision algorithm in reverse. It instructed an ANN to output pictures of the parts of images it was evaluating during the deep-learning process. As Will Knight, senior AI editor at *MIT Technology Review*, explains, the AI, known as Deep Dream, generated "grotesque, alien-like animals emerging from clouds and plants, and hallucinatory pagodas blooming across forests and mountain ranges."[19] While this gave scientists hints about how ANNs recognize patterns, it did not really explain the underlying logic the ANN was using. But it did highlight the fact that ANNs perceive patterns much differently than humans do.

The black box problem has become a real stumbling block for groups that use AI to help make important decisions. For instance, AI is being used more and more by the military. AI sifts through intelligence data, plans routes through dangerous territory, and even drives automated vehicles into combat. But because of the black box problem, military experts have to trust the information that AI provides without knowing the reasoning behind it. This is especially problematic in life-or-death situations. As David Gunning, head of the US military's Explainable Artificial Intelligence program, explains, "It's often the nature of these machine-learning systems that they produce a lot of false alarms, so an intel analyst really needs extra help to understand why a recommendation was made."[20]

Elusive Inner Processes ■

The black box problem also makes it impossible for humans to learn from AI. For example, in 2015 a diagnostic AI called Deep Patient was put to work at Mount Sinai Hospital in New York City to help doctors identify patients who were at risk of developing serious diseases such as cancer and schizophrenia. Deep Patient turned out to be particularly good at its job, but it could not provide information about how it made its predictions. If it could, doctors would be able to advise their patients about risk factors, develop lifesaving screening tests, and even increase their own skill sets.

It may be that understanding the inner workings of ANNs will never be possible. After all, people are notoriously bad at understanding their own decision-making processes. "Even if somebody can give you a reasonable-sounding explanation [for his or her actions], it probably is incomplete, and the same could very well be true for AI," explains computer scientist Jeff Clune. "It might just be part of the nature of intelligence that only part of it is exposed to rational explanation. Some of it is just instinctual, or subconscious, or inscrutable."[21]

It is also possible that the black box problem is simply due to a limitation of the human brain. Humans simply may not be able to grasp the level of complexity that occurs inside an ANN. Either way, since ANNs are getting more complex rather than less, it is unlikely that humans will be able to understand their inner processes any time soon.

Learning and Forgetting ■

Another problem that AI researchers are currently struggling with is catastrophic forgetting. As neuroscientist Shelly Fan explains, "Artificial neural networks . . . learn to master a singular task and call it quits. To learn a new task, it has to reset, wiping out previous memories and starting again from scratch."[22] For example, catastrophic forgetting has been a stumbling block for the developers of Watson, who have retooled the AI many times for many different applications. But Watson cannot apply what it learned on its previous task. For instance, even though Watson learned a great deal about the world when it trained to play *Jeopardy!*, that information was overwritten when it was reprogrammed to assist medical researchers.

Human brains do not work this way. Human learning is cumulative; the brain starts learning at birth and does not stop until death. It constantly refines its huge neural network to integrate new information into its existing knowledge base. And that knowledge base is huge. As Fei-Fei Li explains, "If you consider a child's eyes as a pair of biological cameras, they take one picture about every 200 milliseconds. . . . So by age three, a child would have seen hundreds of millions of pictures of the real world. That's a lot of training examples."[23]

For example, if a three-year-old girl sees a giraffe for the first time in a book of cartoon drawings, her brain automatically compares the giraffe to things she already knows. The giraffe has spots like other animals she has seen, but they are in a new pattern. It looks like a little bit like her dog, but its neck is much longer. If she then goes to the zoo and sees a giraffe, she will most likely recognize it—even though she has only seen a single example of a giraffe in her life.

A young girl will likely recognize a giraffe at the zoo after only seeing one cartoon image of a giraffe in her life. This is because she has access to previous years of accumulated knowledge about the world that aids her thought process.

One of the reasons that a three-year-old girl can recognize a live giraffe after seeing one in a book is because she has access to three years of accumulated knowledge about the world. For instance, she knows the giraffe is an animal because it has four legs and a tail. She also knows that cartoons can represent real things, and she understands the ways in which they appear similar and different. And her brain has mastered the ability of de-prioritizing details that do not matter and picking out details that are important for identification—a process called generalization. In this case she intuitively knows that the important details about the giraffe are its long neck and its unique pattern of spots.

AI systems currently in use—even those with extremely complex neural networks—cannot do this. As science writer Emily Singer explains:

> That superficially easy feat [recognizing a giraffe] is in reality quite sophisticated. The cartoon drawing is a frozen silhouette of simple lines, while the living animal is awash in color, texture, movement and light. It can contort into different shapes and looks different from every angle. Humans excel at this kind of task. We can effortlessly grasp the most important features of an object from just a few examples and apply those features to the unfamiliar. Computers, on the other hand, typically need to sort through a whole database of giraffes, shown in many settings and from different perspectives, to learn to accurately recognize the animal.[24]

The only way to expand AI's current abilities is to solve the problem of catastrophic forgetting. "If we're going to have computer programs that are more intelligent and more useful, then they will have to have this ability to learn sequentially,"[25] explains AI researcher James Kirkpatrick. Until they can, ANNs are destined to be one-trick ponies: systems that cannot synthesize different kinds of information or solve more than one problem at a time.

Reverse Engineering Memory ■

The best hope for solving the problem of catastrophic forgetting is to attempt to reverse engineer the brain's memory center: the hippocampus. The hippocampus stores memories by using brain plasticity. As Fan explains, "In a human, memories undergo a kind of selection: if they help with subsequent learning, they become protected; otherwise, they're erased."[26] In other words, if short-term memories have a future use, the synaptic connections between the neurons involved grow stronger and preserve them in long-term memory.

In 2017 researchers at DeepMind, Google's AI research division, applied this theory to AlphaGo. AlphaGo has the ability to teach itself a variety of computer games, but it could not transfer its knowledge and skills from one game to the next. To solve this problem, researchers programmed AlphaGo to preserve the neural connections that were helpful in learning each game. For instance, after AlphaGo masters one game, it pauses and preserves the things

it has learned that were most important to its success. It can then learn another game and build on the preserved knowledge and skills. This technique, called elastic weight consolidation (EWC), allowed AlphaGo to steadily improve its performance as it learned each new game. However, it still performed worse than it did when it was tasked to learn only a single game. As Kirkpatrick explains, "We have demonstrated that [EWC] can learn tasks sequentially, but we haven't shown that it learns them better because it learns them sequentially."[27] Clearly, EWC needs work, but it might prove to be an innovative solution to the problem of catastrophic forgetting.

Creativity, Computer Style ■

Many people believe that computers will never be advanced enough to be truly creative. This may be because most people have a hard time defining what, exactly, creativity is. John Smith, who works with Watson at IBM, defines creativity as "finding something novel, unexpected, and yet useful."[28] Using that definition, AlphaGo has already demonstrated that AI can come up with creative solutions to difficult problems.

In its match against Lee Sedol, AlphaGo executed a few moves that were so unusual, unexpected, and effective that professional Go players were stunned. As Sedol said after the match, "It made me question human creativity. When I saw AlphaGo's moves, I wondered whether the Go moves I have known were the right ones."[29] However, because AlphaGo's ANN is essentially a black box, experts have no idea how AlphaGo came up with its innovative strategy.

AI Takes on Advertising

The advertising industry is beginning to benefit from the creative abilities of AI. Advertisers attempt to come up with ads that are as attention grabbing as possible, but they must draw on human creativity to design these ads. The ad agency M&C Saatchi London has created an AI algorithm that uses the principles of machine learning and evolution to take over this creative role. The agency designed an outdoor advertising campaign using a digital poster that could determine what elements of an advertisement people paid most attention to.

M&C Saatchi's "smart billboard" was equipped with computer perception that could read the facial expressions of passersby and gauge how long they looked at various elements of the poster. The poster would then refine itself based on this feedback, modifying elements such as images, font, layout, and so forth. In other words, the images on the poster would evolve over time, with the aim of creating the most attention-grabbing and pleasing ad possible. According to David Cox, the chief innovation officer at M&C Saatchi, "It's the first time a poster has been let loose to entirely write itself, based on what works, rather than just what a person thinks may work. We are not suggesting a diminished role for [creativity], but we know technology will be playing a greater part in what we do." Cox believes this type of AI has the potential to act as a coach in creative endeavors such as advertising.

Quoted in Brady Evan Walker, "Artificial Intelligence: The Creative Coach and Colleague," *Insights* (blog), Persado, November 10, 2016. https://persado.com.

Researchers are still trying to make AI behave more creatively, but attempts thus far have produced mixed results. The dominant strategy is to train an AI system with highly regarded examples of a creative form (paintings, pieces of literature, songs, and so on) and then ask it to produce a similar creative work. For instance, in 2016 Smith and his team used Watson to choose scenes for the trailer of an upcoming horror movie called *Morgan*. Watson trained for this project by analyzing a series of successful horror movie trailers. It then analyzed *Morgan* and chose trailer scenes. Almost every scene Watson picked was approved for use in the trailer, and Watson completed the task in a fraction of the time it would have taken a team of professionals to do the same work. While many would not consider this an example of true creativity, Watson was able to do a creative task as well as or better than a human being.

Other researchers have attempted to design AI to create original works of art or pieces of writing. For instance, AI researcher Ross Goodwin created an AI system called Benjamin that could write screenplays. Goodwin trained Benjamin on about a dozen screenplays, and then asked it to write its own. The result, a short film called *Sunspring* that Goodwin then produced, was very unusual. For instance, the opening lines of the film's dialog reads as follows:

> Man: In a future with mass unemployment, young people are forced to sell blood. That's the first thing I can do.
>
> Woman: You should see the boys and shut up. I was the one who was going to be a hundred years old.
>
> Man: I saw him again. The way you were sent to me . . . that was a big honest idea. I am not a bright light.[30]

It is easy for people to read meaning into Benjamin's words, which are both evocative and emotional. But it is very unlikely that Benjamin's ANN is making meaning in a creative way. As Goodwin explains, "Benjamin only creates screenplays based on what other people have written, so by definition it's not really authentic to his voice—it's just a pure reflection of what other people have said."[31]

What Creativity Looks like in the Brain ■

The problems with designing AI that can behave creatively may have to do with how creativity arises in the brain. Studies have revealed that creativity may be a function of turning off certain types of brain activity. For instance, several studies asked musicians to improvise while hooked up to a functional magnetic resonance imaging machine. Scans of their brains revealed that a region called the dorsolateral prefrontal cortex (DLPFC)—an area of the brain involved in planning and self-control—became inactive. In other words, creativity may depend on turning off goal-oriented functions.

In addition, emotions also seem to play a big role in creativity. According to Malinda McPherson, a doctoral candidate at the Harvard-MIT Program in Speech and Hearing Bioscience and Technology, "Emotions have a huge effect on the way our brains can be creative."[32] She led a 2016 study that tested DLPFC activity in musicians who were experiencing happy or sad emotions while improvising and found that happiness seemed to suppress DLPFC activity even further. It is still unclear if emotions are necessary for creativity, but if they are, creativity may be impossible for AI.

If that is the case, then AlphaGo's unusual game play only seemed creative, like the bizarre language in *Sunspring*. Many experts think this is the case and believe that true creativity in a computer system is either impossible or a long way off. As Jason Toy, chief executive officer of the deep-learning company Somatic, asserts, "Can we take what humans think is beautiful and creative and try to put that into an algorithm? I don't think it's going to be possible for quite a while."[33]

AI in general, and deep learning in particular, has a long way to go before it can behave creatively or solve complex problems. However, its ability to perceive its environment, communicate using language, learn, and reason is gradually improving. Optimizing these areas may allow AI to behave more creatively—a crucial part of complex problem solving that may bring researchers one step closer to developing human-level AGI.

CHAPTER 3

SOLUTIONS:
Gain an Understanding of Intelligence

"The rise of powerful AI will be either the best or the worst thing ever to happen to humanity. We do not know which."

—Stephen Hawking, theoretical physicist

Quoted in James Titcomb, "Stephen Hawking Says Artificial Intelligence Could Be Humanity's Greatest Disaster," *Telegraph* (London), October 19, 2016. www.telegraph.co.uk.

Experts agree that humanity is on the brink of an AI revolution. The influx of new AI technologies has the potential to do enormous good—and enormous harm. Autonomous AI (AI that can act independently with very little intervention) could free humanity from nearly all labor, allowing it to focus on more interesting and fulfilling pursuits. It also has the potential—especially in the short term—to throw millions out of work and destroy whole sectors of the economy. In addition, as autonomous AI reaches or surpasses human intelligence, moving from artificial narrow intelligence (ANI) to artificial general intelligence (AGI), it could solve humanity's most vexing problems. On the other hand, some of the world's leading thinkers worry that AGI might one day decide that humans are no longer necessary.

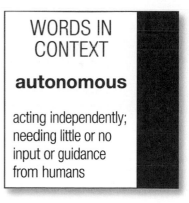

WORDS IN CONTEXT

autonomous

acting independently; needing little or no input or guidance from humans

Experts cannot agree about how long it will take to develop AGI. Some say it is fifty years off at least, while others say it could be developed by 2030. But most are certain that once AGI is

39

developed, it will completely revolutionize life on earth. "Technology will get better fast—and come at us fast," predicts Kevin Maney, technology columnist for *Newsweek*. "AI will lead us into the mother of all tech revolutions."[34]

Because of its potential to transform entire industries, the world's biggest data and technology companies are devoting tremendous resources to be the first to create AGI. The products they have developed have already shifted the world's economy and changed the way people live their lives. But researchers have a long way to go before they discover how to replicate human intelligence. Even though AI can do some things as well as or better than humans, AI systems still cannot learn, reason, or solve problems nearly as well as people can.

Reverse Engineering Intelligence ■
There is a huge stumbling block to the development of AGI, and it does not have to do with reverse engineering the staggering complexity of the human brain. It has to do with the mind. The problem is that scientists do not understand what intelligence actually is. As Microsoft cofounder Paul Allen explains, creating human-level AI "requires a prior scientific understanding of the foundations of human cognition, and we are just scraping the surface of this."[35] AI experts like Allen believe that scientists will never achieve AGI until they understand human intelligence.

Work on reverse engineering intelligence starts with defining the problem. There are several things that psychologists and cognitive scientists think are necessary for an artificial brain to achieve human-level intelligence. The first is data. The second is the ability to synthesize data into concepts. And the third is the ability to organize those concepts in a way that allows them to be processed quickly and efficiently.

The Mind-Body Connection ■
People are exposed to huge amounts of data over their lifetimes. This data comes in through the five senses—sight, sound, touch, taste, and smell—and is experienced by the body. AI researcher Ben Medlock explains:

We think with our whole body, not just with the brain. . . . When a human thinks about a cat, she can probably picture the way it moves, hear the sound of purring, feel the impending scratch from an unsheathed claw. She has a rich store of sensory information at her disposal to understand the idea of a "cat," and other related concepts that might help her interact with such a creature.[36]

By virtue of deep-learning techniques, advanced AI can also take in and process massive amounts of data at tremendous speeds. But because AI cannot experience this data through the senses, it cannot experience anything from an emotional perspective. It does not have feelings that it can attach to sensory input—feelings that deepen and enrich experience in humans. Therefore, even though a computer can gather and process more data than a person, it may ultimately have access

Microsoft cofounder Paul Allen believes that In order to develop human-level artificial intelligence, scientists must first understand the foundations of human cognition and thinking.

to less information because the information it gathers is one-dimensional.

Synthesizing Concepts ■

Another thing that makes intelligence possible is the ability to form concepts. Forming concepts—synthesizing specific knowledge into a generalized understanding—allows people to consolidate data into big, richly nuanced ideas. For example, a door can be large or small, open or closed, locked or unlocked. It is connected to ideas like access, privacy, safety, hospitality, and keeping something out or letting something in. People can apply the rich and varied concept of a door to a variety of things, both practical and metaphorical. Understanding this concept is why a phrase like "you have to knock on a lot of doors to get ahead" is fairly easy for most people to understand.

Concepts allow people to create what Medlock calls "a model of the world." This model is essentially a deep understanding of what things are and how they relate to each other. For instance, in most cases people who understand the concept of a cat and the concept of a door can easily figure out that when a cat cries at a door, it wants to go out—even if it is not their cat and not their door. Because of concepts and models, Medlock explains, "when a human approaches a new problem, most of the hard work has already been done."[37]

WORDS IN CONTEXT

commonsense reasoning

the ability to reason based on general, commonsense knowledge about the world

The human ability to form concepts allows people to use what scientists call commonsense reasoning—which is nothing more than understanding that the cat wants to go out the door. So far, commonsense reasoning has been beyond the abilities of AI. For AI to even recognize a door, it must first view thousands of different types of doors. It must then learn what doors are for—again, by viewing thousands of examples. It must do the same with cats. Even then, unless it also watched a few thousand cats go out a few thousand doors, it still would not understand that the cat wanted out.

The Algorithm That Organizes the Brain ■

Finally, scientists believe that for intelligence to be possible, the human brain must have an orderly way to organize and process data. "Many people have long speculated that there has to be a basic design principle from which intelligence originates and the brain evolves, like how the double helix of DNA and genetic codes are universal for every organism,"[38] explains neuroscientist Joe Tsien. Some researchers believe this basic design principle is responsible for organizing sensory information into concepts. And, like an arrangement of pixels forms an image, it might even spontaneously give rise to intelligence.

In 2016 Tsien found evidence to support this theory, which he dubbed the theory of connectivity—the idea that "a relatively simple mathematical logic underlies our complex brain computations."[39] He discovered a simple algorithm that he believed could predict the number of neurons that will fire in response to sensory input. This algorithm is $N = 2^i - 1$, where i is sensory input and N is the number of groups of neurons that fire in response.

Tsien's algorithm predicted that if he gave rats four different types of food ($i = 4$), then fifteen groups of neurons would fire in response ($N - 15$). He was able to test the formula by implanting electrodes inside the brains of rats and monitoring neural activity. As the algorithm predicted, fifteen clusters of neurons fired in each version of the experiment. These results have been hailed as a breakthrough in the understanding of the way the brain operates.

Tsien's theory is still being tested, but AI researchers are already thinking about how it could be used to organize artificial neural networks (ANNs). While there is much more research to be done, this algorithm might be the key to reverse engineering intelligence and creating AGI.

Autonomous Vehicles ■

The intensive research into AGI has resulted in a flood of ANI technologies entering the market. Even if AGI is never developed, these emerging technologies have the potential to completely revolutionize society. Taking a close look at one such invention, the autonomous vehicle, can reveal some of the amazing—and unsettling—ways that AI will transform the future of humanity.

A Tesla automobile (pictured) has a self-driving feature called Autopilot. Self-driving cars are equipped with some of the most sophisticated artificial intelligence systems developed so far.

Autonomous vehicles, also known as self-driving cars, contain some of the most sophisticated AI systems developed so far. Self-driving cars developed by companies like Tesla Motors and Uber Technologies are equipped with computer-perception systems that perceive the environment far better than any human driver. For instance, the Tesla is equipped with cameras that provide 360-degree vision, ultrasonic sensors that can detect hard and soft objects in the roadway, and radar with enhanced processing that can navigate safely in rain, fog, dust, and other atmospheric conditions. According to Tesla's website, this computer-perception system "provides a view of the world that a driver alone cannot access, seeing in every direction simultaneously and on wavelengths that go far beyond the human senses."[40]

The AI that powers the Tesla, called Autopilot, has been extensively trained using deep-learning techniques, but it also uses vast amounts of incoming sensory data to continuously learn about its environment. In addition, the Tesla shares sensor data with other Teslas on the road. This means that the Tesla is continuously updated about driving conditions and traffic. It also means that Autopilot can learn from data collected by all Teslas—which have driven well over 222 million miles so far.

Self-driving cars have been on the roads since 2015, but they require an alert driver who must still perform some driving duties. However, truly autonomous vehicles are nearly ready for the road. The cofounder of Tesla, Elon Musk, announced that Tesla vehicles are now fully capable of being completely autonomous. However, because Autopilot still needs to be refined, this feature is not fully activated. Instead, the new Tesla is set to operate in shadow mode, which means that the cars will wirelessly send data back to the company so that Autopilot can learn from this data and improve itself. Musk also stated that the company planned to complete a fully autonomous test drive from Los Angeles to New York by the end of 2017 "without the need for a single touch, including the charger."[41] His goal is to be able to offer autonomous driving to the public by 2019.

A World Without Drivers

As self-driving cars become fully autonomous, they have the potential to radically improve society. Worldwide, car crashes kill over 1.3 million people every year. Experts predict that widespread use of self-driving cars will eliminate 90 percent of auto accidents and save $190 billion in damages and related health care costs. In addition, because the AI in these vehicles will share data about traffic flow, most traffic delays will be eliminated, optimizing travel time and saving fuel.

Experts also believe self-driving cars will change society's infrastructure—especially in cities. For instance, cities will no longer need to delegate space for parking; self-driving cars can simply

Are Self-Driving Cars Safe?

There have been several high-profile accidents involving self-driving cars. For instance, in May 2016 a Tesla equipped with both Autopilot and a manual override system was involved in a fatal tractor-trailer accident. According to a statement issued by Tesla, "Neither Autopilot nor the driver noticed the white side of the tractor trailer against a brightly lit sky, so the brake was not applied." The Tesla's computer-vision system was unable to identify the slight change in color as an obstacle, and the car attempted to drive under the tractor trailer, killing the occupant.

Such incidents have made the public understandably skeptical about the safety of self-driving cars. Yet Elon Musk asserts that, from a statistical stand-point, the Tesla Autopilot feature is already much safer than a human driver. "In the distant future," he says, "people may outlaw driving cars because it's too dangerous. You can't have a person driving a two-ton death machine."

Tesla, "A Tragic Loss," June 30, 2016. www.tesla.com.

Quoted in Phil LeBeau, "Musk: Someday, Driving a Car Will Be Illegal," CNBC, March 17, 2015. www.cnbc.com.

drop off their passengers and go to a designated waiting area at the edge of the city. Self-driving cars are also likely to replace the current public transportation system, making car ownership unnecessary for many people. Finally, self-driving cars will have a huge impact on quality of life, since people will be able to engage in other activities while in their cars. As Uber's founder Travis Kalanick explains, when this is combined with the reduction in traffic and commuting time, "trillions of hours will be given back to people—quality of life goes way up."[42]

There will be significant costs to the adaption of self-driving cars, however—mostly in the form of jobs lost. Driving is a popular job in the United States, and it is one of the few careers that can provide people who do not have a college degree with a middle-class income. Self-driving cars would eliminate these jobs, throwing 4.1 million drivers out of work, according to the financial website MarketWatch. Industries that are related to driving will also be impacted. For instance, automotive engineers who work at optimizing the driving experience will no longer be needed, and fewer police will be required to patrol the roads. In summary, self-driving cars are a prime example of a new AI technology that has the potential to completely change society in the near future—for good and for ill.

The End of Work ■

Self-driving cars are a good example of how further developments in AI will transform people's lives. But compared to what AI has the potential to do, self-driving cars are just the beginning. In fact, experts believe that AI will eventually be able to do 90 percent of all human labor on the planet—long before AGI is a reality. This is because the more specialized the task, the easier it is for AI to replicate it. "A computer doesn't need to replicate the entire spectrum of your intellectual capability in order to displace you from your job," explains Martin Ford, author of *Rise of the Robots: Technology and the Threat of a Jobless Future*. "It only needs to do the specific things you are paid to do."[43]

Specialized tasks are algorithmic—they are based on a complex sequence of behaviors that can often be translated into a computer algorithm. According to Oxford University researchers Carl Benedikt Frey and Michael Osborne, about 47 percent of jobs in the United States are algorithmic and may be lost to AI by 2033. Professions that have a high probability (more than 70 percent) of being taken over by AI include insurance underwriters, paralegals, office clerks, cashiers, chefs and waiters, construction laborers and carpenters, and security guards.

Even occupations that require a great deal of training could be taken over by AI. For instance, IBM's Watson can already read imaging data better than a doctor, and many surgeries are already performed with assistance from robots. These emerging technologies are often better at these specialized tasks than people because they eliminate human error. As computer scientist Geoffrey Hinton predicts, "It's just completely obvious that in five years deep learning is going to do better than radiologists. . . . They should stop training radiologists now."[44]

Will AGI Save the World? ■

If the coming AI revolution is likely to disrupt society, the invention of AGI is likely to repair it. Human-level AGI will have the reasoning and problem-solving ability of a human while being immune to things like bias, information overload, forgetfulness, the need for sleep, and any other human issue that could cause an error in reasoning. In other words, AGI will most likely be able to figure out a solution to any problems ANI is likely to cause.

In fact, AGI has the potential to solve all of the problems that humanity struggles with. As Demis Hassabis, chief executive officer of Google DeepMind, explains, the underlying goal of the quest for AGI is to use it to tackle the world's grand challenges. "If we can solve intelligence in a general enough way," he says, "then we can apply it to all sorts of things to make the world a better place."[45] For instance, AGI has the potential to figure out ways to optimize economic systems, create stable and just governments, and do long-term planning to ensure the survival of the planet. It could also invent technologies that would allow us to eliminate pollution, colonize other worlds, increase our own intelligence, or even extend our lives indefinitely. As chief technology officer of Facebook Mike Schroepfer explains, "The power of AI technology is it can solve problems that scale to the whole planet."[46]

Our Last Invention ■

Many AI theorists believe that human-level AGI will be humanity's final grand invention. This is because as soon as people create AGI that is as smart as a human being, it will be able to improve itself. As AI researcher Ben Goertzel explains, "You can teach this human level AGI math and programming and AI theory and cognitive science and neuroscience. This human level AGI can then reprogram itself and it can modify its own mind and it can make itself into a yet smarter machine."[47] In other words, in much the same way that deep learning allows AI to learn autonomously, AGI would be able to improve itself autonomously, increasing its intelligence at an exponential rate and giving itself the ability to invent more and more advanced

Will AI Cause Chaos in Society?

If millions of workers lose their jobs because of rapidly advancing AI, society could be thrown into chaos. As economist Carlota Perez, who has studied the effect of new technologies on society, explains, "A society that had established countless routines and habits, norms and regulations, to fit the conditions of the previous revolution, does not find it easy to assimilate the new one."

Change can be both difficult and frightening, but people tend to adapt. And by looking at how technology has impacted society throughout history, it is clear that every technological revolution has created more wealth for the average person than it displaces. History has shown that automation caused a rise in literacy rates and standards of living. It also caused crime rates to fall and average life spans to lengthen.

Experts believe that if the AI revolution is planned for and managed—perhaps by sharing the wealth created with those who are displaced by AI-driven technologies—the disruptive effect on society could be limited. As former president Barack Obama notes, "If properly harnessed, it [AI] can generate enormous prosperity and opportunity. But it also has some downsides that we're gonna have to figure out."

Quoted in Kevin Maney, "How Artificial Intelligence and Robots Will Radically Transform the Economy," *Newsweek*, November 30, 2016. www.newsweek.com.

Quoted in Scott Dadich, "Barack Obama, Neural Nets, Self-Driving Cars, and the Future of the World," *Wired*, 2016. www.wired.com.

technologies. Goertzel imagines these advanced AGI entities as "superhuman minds":

> If you have a million times human IQ and you can reconfigure elementary particles into new forms of matter at will then supplying a few billion humans with food and water and video games, virtual reality headsets and national parks and flying cars and what not—this would be trivial for these superhuman minds. . . . You don't have to work for a living. You can devote your time to social, emotional,

spiritual, intellectual and creative pursuits rather than laboriously doing things you might rather not do just in order to get food and shelter and an internet connection. So I think there is tremendous positive possibilities here.[48]

Is AGI Safe? ■

Goertzel is not the only person who believes that as soon as humans achieve AGI and give computers the ability to improve themselves, intelligence in artificial systems will increase at an exponential rate. But not everyone is optimistic about the outcome. Some of the world's top thinkers are extremely concerned about artificial superintelligence. Elon Musk has described it as "our biggest existential threat."[49] Theoretical physicist Stephen Hawking warns, "The development of full artificial intelligence could spell the end of the human race."[50] In fact, in 2015 concerned scientists wrote a document called "Research Priorities for Robust and Beneficial Artificial Intelligence: An Open Letter" that expresses the concern that "we could one day lose control of AI systems via the rise of superintelligences that do not act in accordance with human wishes—and that such powerful systems would threaten humanity."[51] Along with Musk and Hawking, hundreds of scientists who work with AI have signed the letter, including leaders at Google, Facebook, Microsoft, IBM, Apple, and dozens of universities.

These scientists want to be sure that—as philosopher Nick Bostrom puts it—AI is designed to be "fundamentally on our side." Bostrom explains that, because AI is designed to be goal seeking, a superintelligent AI would be "extremely good at using available means to achieve a state in which its goal is realized." He gives what he calls a "cartoon example" of this: "Suppose we give A.I. the goal to solve a difficult mathematical problem. When the A.I. becomes superintelligent, it realizes that the most effective way to get the solution to this problem is by transforming the planet into a giant computer, so as to increase its thinking capacity. . . . Human beings in this model are threats, we could prevent the mathematical problem from being solved."[52] Bostrom believes the way to avoid this type of situation is to give AI human values and design it to be motivated to help us. AGI could even use machine-learning techniques to study human values and program itself to align with them, he says.

Theoretical physicist Stephen Hawking (pictured) believes that the realization of full artificial intelligence could spell the end of the human race.

Other scientists disagree that AGI will ever be a threat to humanity. For instance, astrophysicist Neil deGrasse Tyson says, "Seems to me, as long as we don't program emotions into robots, there's no reason to fear them taking over the world."[53] Tyson and other experts think that people fear AGI because they are envisioning it as a superintelligent version of a human—in other words, a being that has the potential to act aggressively or selfishly. But computers are made to do what they are programmed to do, Tyson says. Building in some simple safeguards should prevent them from accidentally doing harm.

The AGI Revolution Is Coming ■

AGI has the potential to change society—and perhaps humanity itself—completely, irrevocably, and in ways experts cannot yet imagine. Some of those changes may be destructive, while others may literally save the planet. Even though researchers are nowhere near creating a human-like AI, most are certain that AGI is coming—and sooner than most people think.

CHAPTER 4

SOLUTIONS:
Combine Human and Artificial Intelligence

"I think if humanity were to identify a singular thing to work on, the thing that would demand the greatest minds of our generation, it's human intelligence, specifically, the ability to co-evolve with artificial intelligence."

—Bryan Johnson, founder of the neuroscience company Kernel

Quoted in Nick Statt, "Kernel Is Trying to Hack the Human Brain—but Neuroscience Has a Long Way to Go," Verve, February 22, 2017. www.theverge.com.

Elon Musk has expressed considerable concern about AGI and how it might be dangerous to humanity. But rather than warning people away from AGI research, he is encouraging development in a different area of AI. Musk believes that the safest—and the most promising—way to design AI is to make it support and enhance human intelligence. "If the AIs are all separate, vastly more intelligent than us," Musk says, "how do you ensure that they don't have optimization functions that are contrary to the best interests of humanity?" Musk's answer to this question is to make sure that humans are central to AI development, rather than allowing AI to replace humans. In the future, he believes, human brains will merge with AI technology— possibly leading to the creation of cyborgs. In this way, he says, "AI wouldn't be 'other'—it would be you."[54]

WORDS IN CONTEXT

augmentation

to improve the way something functions or add value to something that already exists

What Is Intelligence Augmentation? ■

The approach that Musk is advocating is well established—it is known as intelligence augmentation (or cognitive augmentation or machine-augmented intelligence). Intelligence augmentation is a robust field of AI research that attempts to find ways to enhance the human brain with AI technology. It seeks to find ways for AI and human intelligence to complement each other by making up for each other's shortcomings. "Tasks that seem laborious to us . . . are easy for a computer," explains neuroscientist Kelly Clancy, "whereas those that seem easy to us . . . have been the hardest for A.I. to master."[55] Intelligence augmentation brings the best of human and artificial intelligence together.

Elon Musk (pictured) believes that the best and safest way to develop artificial intelligence is to make it support and enhance human thought rather than try to replace it.

Computers excel at synthesizing information quickly and accurately. However, they have trouble making sense of that information—especially when a conclusion calls for common-sense reasoning. Humans, on the other hand, excel at common-sense reasoning and can form conclusions quickly. The problem is, they often base their conclusions on incomplete or biased information. "We confuse the easily imaginable with the highly probable, let emotions cloud judgments, find patterns in random noise, . . . and overgeneralize from personal experience," write AI researchers Jim Guszcza, Harvey Lewis, and Peter Evans-Greenwood. The idea behind intelligence augmentation is that AI should be used as a tool, providing data so humans can make the best decision possible. "Minds need algorithms to de-bias our judgments and decisions as surely as our eyes need artificial lenses to see adequately," the researchers explain. "With intelligence augmentation, the ultimate goal is not building machines that think like humans, but designing machines that help humans think better."[56]

Intelligence augmentation is not just used to help people make good decisions; it can partner with humans in other ways. For instance, AI researcher Maurice Conti works with a type of intelligence augmentation called generative AI—AI that helps people generate designs. "I want to say, 'Computer, let's design a car,' and the computer shows me a car. And I say, 'No, more fast-looking, and less German,' and bang, the computer shows me an option," Conti says. He explains that generative AI can "come up with new designs all by themselves. All it needs are your goals and your constraints."[57]

Conti has been using generative AI to design a new type of plane in partnership with Airbus. For instance, Airbus engineers needed to create interior walls that were both very light and very strong. Given these parameters, Conti's generative AI produced a perforated panel that was stronger than the original but half its weight—and which could be created with a 3-D printer. Airbus has already integrated this partition into its fleet.

Elon Musk

Elon Musk is an investor, engineer, inventor, and futurist. He has founded several innovative technology companies, including the online money transfer service PayPal; the space exploration company SpaceX, which is attempting to create reusable rockets that will make it possible for humans to colonize Mars; Tesla Motors, the electric car company that is leading the quest to develop self-driving vehicles; and OpenAI, a nonprofit AI research company that aims to develop freely available AI in a way that is safe and beneficial to humanity. Musk's newest AI venture, Neuralink, has the goal of developing brain-machine interfaces—devices that connect the human brain and merge biological and artificial intelligence.

Almost all of Musk's companies are designed to encourage technological development in a way that will, in Musk's opinion, benefit humanity in the long run. As science communicator Tim Urban explains, "When Elon builds a company, its core initial strategy is usually to create the match that will ignite the industry and get the . . . [world] working on the cause. This, in turn, Elon believes, will lead to developments that will change the world in the way that increases the likelihood of humanity having the best possible future." This, Urban says, is Musk's reason for creating Neuralink. Musk believes humanity has the best chance of long-term survival if it embraces augmented intelligence, which is the ultimate blending of human and artificial intelligence.

Tim Urban, "Neuralink and the Brain's Magical Future," *Wait but Why* (blog), April 20, 2017. http://wait butwhy.com.

Another type of intelligence augmentation involves giving intelligence to robots that can do repetitive tasks faster and more accurately than humans. In Conti's applied research lab, his team has developed an AI robot called Bishop, which was teamed with a construction worker. "Bishop's human partner can tell [it] what to do in plain English and with simple gestures, kind of like talking to a dog, and then Bishop executes on those instructions with perfect precision," Conti explains. "We're using the human for what the human is good at: awareness, perception and decision making. And we're using the robot for what it's good at: precision and repetitiveness." Bishop can also act as a project manager, directing humans to do tasks that are currently too hard for a robot to do. Conti describes one such project where a team was tasked to build a complex pavilion in three days: He said Bishop "was telling the humans what to do, telling the robots what to do and keeping track of thousands of individual components. What's interesting is, building this pavilion [so quickly] was simply not possible without human, robot and AI augmenting each other."[58]

These are just some of the possibilities when AI is used to augment, rather than replace, human intelligence. However, intelligence augmentation researchers are interested in doing more than just creating robots or AI systems that work in partnership with humans. They want to build technology that physically interfaces with the human body, augmenting intelligence at its source—the brain.

Brain-Machine Interfaces ■

Brain-machine interfaces (BMIs), also known as brain-computer interfaces, are physical devices that connect to the brain. Their purpose is to enhance cognitive function or to repair or replace a damaged brain system. For instance, one type of BMI is called a neurostimulator—a computer chip that is implanted into the brain that directly stimulates neurons that are no longer firing. Neurostimulators have been in use for decades to treat Parkinson's disease and other brain-based disorders. Another type of BMI is called a neuroprosthetic. Neuroprosthetics have been around since 1957, when the first cochlear implant was developed. The cochlear implant is a device surgically implanted in the ear that converts sound waves into electronic signals that are picked up by the brain and interpreted as sound. Vision neuroprosthetics, which help blind people see, work in the same way as the cochlear implant—they act as a bridge between the eye and the brain, translating sensory input into electrical impulses.

Neuroprosthetics can also form a bridge between the brain and nervous system in the opposite direction, transforming electrical impulses generated by the brain into motor activity. For instance, by targeting neurons in the brain that control various body movements, neuroprosthetics allow people with disabilities to move artificial limbs with their minds. These types of neuroprosthetics usually consist of a tiny chip that is implanted in the brain and is connected to the neurons that control movement. The chip intercepts signals from the neurons (which fire when a person tries to move a limb) and sends them to a robotic prosthesis (such as an artificial arm or leg that is equipped with robotic hardware and software). Sometimes these robot prostheses are equipped with sensors that transmit the sensation of touch back to the brain. For instance, in 2016 a paralyzed man named Nathan Copeland was the first to control a sensor-equipped robotic arm with his mind. The arm was not attached to his body; it was mounted to a platform beside him. "I can feel just about every finger," said Copeland. "Sometimes it feels electrical, and sometimes its pressure. . . . It feels like my fingers are getting touched or pushed."[59] Because Copeland can "feel" his robot arm, he can operate it with much greater precision. As biomedical engineer Robert Gaunt explains, Copeland will be able to "pick something up that's soft and not squash it or drop it."[60]

Outsourcing the Brain ■

Currently, BMIs and neuroprosthetics can only help the brain control motor functions. However, researchers have a much loftier goal: They want to create an artificial neocortex that can be connected to the brain with a BMI. The neocortex is the outer layer of the brain responsible for higher functions like learning and reasoning. An artificial neocortex would assist the brain by boosting the power of the neocortex. As futurist Dr. Peter Diamandis explains,

WORDS IN CONTEXT

neocortex

the outer layer of the mammalian brain responsible for higher functions like learning, reasoning, and problem solving

researchers face many challenges creating this type of technology. He says they must first answer these questions:

> Can we mimic the natural function of neurons firing? . . . Could we improve that circuitry? . . . Could we make certain memories stronger? Could we make certain memories weaker? Could we work with neural code in the same way we work with biological code via synthetic biology or genetic code? How do we read and write to neurons? Could we merge with AIs?[61]

Companies like Elon Musk's new venture, Neuralink, are exploring these very questions. They envision a future in which humans will merge with AI through a BMI. This type of technology will be revolutionary. It will let people access the world's information, modify their sensory experiences, and boost their own brain power simply by using their minds to activate an implanted BMI.

AI researcher and futurist Ray Kurzweil believes technology will have advanced enough to make this possible by the 2030s. He predicts that by then, humans will have developed a synthetic neocortex that exists in the cloud for all to access. He gives an example of how this will be used:

> In the 2030s, if you need some extra neocortex, you'll be able to connect to that in the cloud directly from your brain. So I'm walking along and I say, "Oh, there's Chris Anderson. He's coming my way. I'd better think of something clever to say. I've got three seconds. My 300 million modules in my neocortex isn't going to cut it. I need a billion more." I'll be able to access that in the cloud. And our thinking, then, will be a hybrid of biological and non-biological thinking.[62]

This concept tends to make people very nervous. The idea of an outside entity intruding on the brain can cause people to worry that they will lose control of their free will or that their essential self will be changed. Musk explains that this will not be the case—he claims that while a cloud-based AI will give people access to vast amounts of information and enhance their cognitive abilities, it will "feel like it's a part of you."[63] In other words, just like looking something up on the Internet adds to knowledge and taking a stimulating drug like caffeine increases focus, connecting to a cloud-based AI intelligence will simply enhance overall cognitive ability.

Mapping the Brain ■
To interface with the brain in the way Musk and Kurzweil envision, much more must be learned about how the brain works. To that end, several efforts to map the human brain—to tease out all the connections between neurons and understand how they commu-

nicate with each other—are currently underway. For instance, the Human Connectome Project seeks to create a computer simulation of all the connections in the human brain. Such a simulation would not only aid understanding of how neurons communicate, it would allow computers to run whole-brain simulations to test the effects of drugs and other medical interventions.

Perhaps the most ambitious brain-mapping endeavor so far is the Machine Intelligence from Cortical Networks (MICrONS) project. This project, which is part of the Brain Research through Advancing Innovative Neurotechnologies initiative, seeks to translate the connections between neurons into algorithms that can be used in machine learning. MICrONS is mainly concerned with mapping the visual cortex and hopes to use its findings to help AI learn through computer vision, but its results will be applicable to all forms of AI. The knowledge gained from mapping the brain will be especially useful to BMIs.

How Complex Is the Brain? ■

The MICrONS project's initial goal, which is still several years away, is to map 1 cubic millimeter of a mouse's neocortex. This

President Obama speaks about the Brain Research through Advancing Innovative Neurotechnologies (BRAIN) initiative in 2013. One of its goals is to translate the connections between human neurons into algorithms to be used in machine learning.

may not sound like much of an achievement, but if MICrONS succeeds it will be a huge leap forward in researchers' efforts to create both AGI and the type of BMI that Musk and Kurzweil envision. According to Tim Urban, a popular blogger and science communicator, "What makes BMIs so hard is that the engineering challenges are monumental. It's physically working with the brain that makes BMIs among the hardest engineering endeavors in the world."[64] The issue is complexity—the brain is so complex that it is nearly impossible to imagine.

BMIs Help Locked-In Syndrome

Locked-in syndrome is a medical condition in which the body is paralyzed but consciousness and brain function remains unaffected. Some people with locked-in syndrome can still move some facial muscles. AI technologies have been developed that allow these people to communicate by controlling NLP systems with their cheek muscles. However, others who suffer from locked-in syndrome have no control of facial muscles and have no way to communicate with the outside world.

In 2016 a neuroengineering company in Switzerland developed a BMI that allowed people with complete locked-in syndrome to communicate. The BMI is made up of sensors on a cap that sits on top of the head; the sensors precisely pinpoint blood oxygenation levels in the brain. Blood oxygenation increases when neurons are activated. Researchers use this technology to help them map which neurons are associated with different types of brain functions.

At first, locked-in patients were asked to think "yes" or "no" so the device could pinpoint how neurons in their brains fired in response to these thoughts. Once the device was trained, patients were able to answer simple yes or no questions by thinking. Surprisingly, when the patients who tested the device were asked "Are you happy?," all four answered "Yes." Researchers hope that this new technology will one day be able to treat a wide variety of brain-based motor disorders.

Quoted in Kurzweil Accelerating Intelligence, "Brain-Computer Interface Enables Completely Locked-In Patients to Communicate for the First Time," February 2, 2017. www.kurzweilai.net.

Urban attempts to help his readers envision this complexity by asking them to imagine that the neocortex is one thousand times bigger than it is. If this enlarged neocortex was spread out, it would cover about thirty-six city blocks. In just 1 cubic meter of this area (which is about the size of four large trash cans arranged in a cube) there are forty thousand to one hundred thousand neurons, each about the size of a marble. Each marble has between one hundred and ten thousand threadlike structures radiating out from it, which look like strings of spaghetti. Some of the spaghetti strings can be more than half a mile (up to 1 km) long, winding through the city blocks and connecting with other spaghetti strings at junctures called synapses—the places where neurons communicate. According to Urban, in the cubic meter he is describing, there are about 20 million of these synapses. Urban writes, "That means that if we were trying to record signals or stimulate neurons in this particular cubic area, we'd have a lot of difficulty, because in the mess of spaghetti, it would be very hard to figure out which spaghetti strings belonged to our . . . marbles." And, Urban explains, because of brain plasticity, "the tens of millions of synapse connections in our cube would be regularly changing sizes, disappearing, and reappearing."[65]

All of this, Urban emphasizes, actually occurs not in 1 cubic meter but in 1 cubic millimeter of the brain—which is about the size of a grain of sand and the volume that MICrONS hopes to map. Considering that about a half a million grains of sand could be packed into the neocortex, it becomes clear why mapping the entire brain is so difficult.

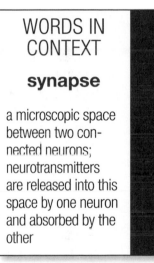

WORDS IN CONTEXT

synapse

a microscopic space between two connected neurons; neurotransmitters are released into this space by one neuron and absorbed by the other

Technology That Sees into the Brain ■

Recent advances in technology—from new techniques that observe neurons in action to new devices that can interface with the brain—are making projects like MICrONS possible. According to Kurzweil, the amount of data neuroscientists are able to detect in the brain is doubling every year, as is the resolution of various imaging technologies. As he explains, "We can now see inside a living brain and see individual interneural connections connecting in real time, firing in real time. We can see your brain create your thoughts. We can see your thoughts create your brain."[66]

For instance, in MICrONS's current effort to map the brain of mice, it uses specialized robots that cut brain tissue into slices that are thinner than a human hair. Laser-based microscopes then create images of the connections among the neurons within the slices. With new computer-modeling technology, the pictures of these slices are then put together in a 3-D image that reveals the complex structure of the brain and allows scientists to trace how neurons connect. In addition, DNA microarrays—chemical detectors that tell scientists what genes are turned on or off in a neuron—help identify the different types of neurons that exist within the slices of brain. So far, more than one thousand different types have been discovered.

Scientists working with living brains have new technologies at their disposal as well. Electrodes are now small enough that thousands can be implanted in the brain of a living laboratory animal. And neural probes that measure neuron activity are now so thin and flexible that they can be inserted directly into brain tissue without causing scar tissue buildup. In addition, genes containing fluorescent proteins can now be inserted into living neurons. These genes can then be turned on and off with special types of light, allowing scientists to make the neuron fire and see the brain's circuitry in action.

On the Cutting Edge of BMI Technology ■

Even with these remarkable advances in technology, scientists will have significant hurdles to overcome before they can implant a BMI device in the brain that can interact with neurons at the level that Musk and Kurzweil envision. For instance, scientists must find a way to make the components of such a device smaller and more power efficient. They must also increase the bandwidth—or the flow of information—of everything from electrodes to artificial neurons. Any BMI device must also be biocompatible with brain tissue so it is not rejected, and it must be able to be implanted without major surgery. Finally, the device itself must be bidirectional—in other words, it must be able to both talk and listen to brain signals.

There are several technologies under development that may solve some of these problems. The first is a BMI called neural lace.

Neural lace was imagined by science fiction writer Iain M. Banks back in 1987, but scientists have seized on the idea and are starting to develop the technology. Essentially, neural lace is a fine, thin mesh that sits on top of the neocortex, creating an interface between the brain and an external AI. Researchers have created a rudimentary form of this lace and tested it on live mice. The mice tolerated the lace well; in fact, as researchers hoped, their

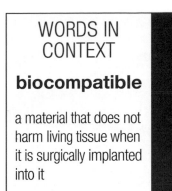

brain cells grew around the mesh, forming biological connections. Neural lace for use in the human brain is currently being researched by two neuroscience start-ups: Kernel, founded by Bryan Johnson, and Elon Musk's Neuralink. Both companies plan to develop neural lace implants to help people with degenerative brain disease restore brain function, but ultimately they hope to use neural lace in healthy people to allow them to connect with AI.

Another exciting new technology currently under development is the artificial synapse. To understand how an artificial synapse works, it is necessary to understand how scientists think a biological synapse gives rise to thought. A synapse is the place where neurons meet. As neuroscientist Shelly Fan explains, a synapse "looks a bit like a battery cell, with two membranes and a gap between." An electrical charge builds up at one side of the synapse and eventually fires. Each time it does, the synapse itself changes its connective state—which is the amount of energy it needs to fire the next time.

As Fan explains, "Neuroscientists believe that different conductive states are how synapses store information."[67] In other words, thoughts and memories may be generated by the connective state of synapses. Since there are trillions of synapses in the brain, and each one can exist in hundreds of different connective states, there are an innumerable number of unique combinations of synapses in various connective states. To better understand this idea, if one thinks of a synapse as a musical instrument, then each note that instrument can play is like a different connective state. Scientists theorize that when a unique combination of synapses fire together, a thought is generated—much like when an orchestra plays a unique combination of notes, a piece of music is generated.

This rendering shows an artificial connection to a human neural network. Scientists hope that concepts like these will be developed and used in the future to enhance human thinking and computational power.

The artificial synapse is designed like a biological synapse. It is made of flexible organic material that can be changed, via electrical charges, into hundreds of different conductive states—just like a biological synapse. It is energy efficient, biocompatible with human tissue, and extremely flexible. The hope is that these artificial synapses could be used to make ANNs that are brain compatible. "[This] opens up a possibility of interfacing live biological cells [with circuits] that can do computing via artificial synapses,"[68] explains AI researcher A. Alec Talin, one of the authors of a study that tested the device's performance. In other words, the brain's neurons could use these artificial synapses to enhance their computational power.

Artificial synapses are in the early stage of development, and they must be made smaller, faster, and more energy efficient, but the technology shows great promise. "We think that could have huge implications in the future for creating much better brain-machine interfaces,"[69] Talin states.

A New Era ◼

There is little doubt that AI will play a defining role in humanity's future. Superintelligent AGI may relieve humans of labor and solve problems that threaten the planet's existence—or it might cause more problems than it solves. Augmented intelligence might allow humans to merge with AI and supercharge their intelligence. Or both types of AI might be developed in tandem, interacting with each other in ways that futurists cannot yet imagine. In any case one thing is clear—a new era has begun, and at its heart is artificial intelligence.

SOURCE NOTES

INTRODUCTION
Is the Brain a Supercomputer?

1. Robert Epstein, "The Empty Brain," *Aeon,* May 18, 2016. https://aeon.co.

2. Gary Marcus, "Face It, Your Brain Is a Computer," *New York Times*, June 27, 2015. www.nytimes.com.

CHAPTER 1
CURRENT STATUS: The Golden Age of Artificial Intelligence

3. *Merriam-Webster Online Dictionary*, "Artificial Intelligence," 2017. www.merriam-webster.com.

4. Quoted in Gil Press, "Artificial Intelligence Defined as a New Research Discipline: This Week in Tech History," *Forbes*, August 28, 2016. www.forbes.com.

5. Quoted in Gideon Lewis-Kraus, "The Great A.I. Awakening," *New York Times,* December 14, 2016. www.nytimes.com.

6. Lewis-Kraus, "The Great A.I. Awakening."

7. Bernard Marr, "Are Artificial Intelligence and Machine Learning the Same Thing?," LinkedIn, January 18, 2017. www.linked in.com.

8. Amazon Web Services, "What Is Artificial Intelligence?," 2017. https://aws.amazon.com.

9. Fei-Fei Li, "How We're Teaching Computers to Understand Pictures," TED, March 2015. www.ted.com.

10. Lewis-Kraus, "The Great A.I. Awakening."

11. Robin Sandhu, "Applications of Natural Language Processing Technology," Lifewire, April 22, 2017. www.lifewire.com.

12. Lewis-Kraus, "The Great A.I. Awakening."

13. Quoted in Jonathan Holmes, "AI Is Already Making Inroads into Journalism but Could It Win a Pulitzer?," *Guardian* (Manchester), April 3, 2016. www.theguardian.com.

14. Kris Hammond, "What Is Artificial Intelligence?," *Computerworld*, April 10, 2015. www.computerworld.com.
15. Hammond, "What Is Artificial Intelligence?"
16. Jo Best, "IBM Watson: The Inside Story of How the *Jeopardy*-Winning Supercomputer Was Born, and What It Wants to Do Next," TechRepublic, September 9, 2013. www.techrepublic.com.
17. Quoted in Mary Chris Jaklevic, "MD Anderson Cancer Center's IBM Watson Project Fails, and So Did the Journalism Related to It," Health News Review, February 23, 2017. www.healthnewsreview.org.

CHAPTER 2
LIMITATIONS: Why Artificial Intelligence Is Not Smarter—Yet

18. Quoted in Will Knight, "The Dark Secret at the Heart of AI," *MIT Technology Review*, April 11, 2017. www.technologyreview.com.
19. Knight, "The Dark Secret at the Heart of AI."
20. Quoted in Knight, "The Dark Secret at the Heart of AI."
21. Quoted in Knight, "The Dark Secret at the Heart of AI."
22. Shelly Fan, "Google Chases General Intelligence with New AI That Has a Memory," Singularity Hub, March 29, 2017. https://singularityhub.com.
23. Li, "How We're Teaching Computers to Understand Pictures."
24. Emily Singer, "Mapping the Brain to Build Better Machines," *Quanta Magazine*, April 6, 2016. www.quantamagazine.org.
25. Quoted in Fan, "Google Chases General Intelligence with New AI That Has a Memory."
26. Fan, "Google Chases General Intelligence with New AI That Has a Memory."
27. Quoted in Fan, "Google Chases General Intelligence with New AI That Has a Memory."
28. Quoted in IBM, "The Quest for AI Creativity." www.ibm.com.
29. Quoted in David Vandegrift, "Can Artificial Intelligence Be Creative?," Medium, June 9, 2016. https://medium.com.
30. Quoted in "*Sunspring*—a Sci-Fi Short Film Starring Thomas Middleditch," YouTube, June 9, 2016. www.youtube.com.

31. Quoted in Annalee Newitz, "Movie Written by Algorithm Turns Out to Be Hilarious and Intense," Ars Technica, June 9, 2016. https://arstechnica.com.
32. Quoted in Kylah Goodfellow Klinge, "Mapping Creativity in the Brain," *Atlantic*, March 21, 2016. www.theatlantic.com.
33. Quoted in Laura DeLallo, "I Spent a Month in the Minds of AI Experts. Here's What I Learned. . . ," Medium, March 1, 2017. https://medium.com.

CHAPTER 3
SOLUTIONS: Gain an Understanding of Intelligence

34. Kevin Maney, "How Artificial Intelligence and Robots Will Radically Transform the Economy," *Newsweek*, November 30, 2016. www.newsweek.com.
35. Quoted in Clara Lu, "Why We Are Still Light Years Away from Full Artificial Intelligence," TechCrunch, December 14, 2016. https://techcrunch.com.
36. Ben Medlock, "The Body Is the Missing Link for Truly Intelligent Machines," *Aeon*, March 14, 2017. https://aeon.co.
37. Medlock, "The Body Is the Missing Link for Truly Intelligent Machines."
38. Quoted in Aaron Krumins, "Scientists Discover Nature's Algorithm for Intelligence," ExtremeTech, December 8, 2016. www.extremetech.com.
39. Quoted in Krumins, "Scientists Discover Nature's Algorithm for Intelligence."
40. Tesla, "All Tesla Cars Being Produced Now Have Full Self-Driving Hardware," October 19, 2016. www.tesla.com.
41. Quoted in Darrell Etherington, "Musk Targeting Coast-to-Coast Test Drive of Fully Self-Driving Tesla by Late 2017," TechCrunch, October 19, 2016. https://techcrunch.com.
42. Quoted in Biz Carson, "Travis Kalanick on Uber's Bet on Self-Driving Cars: 'I Can't Be Wrong,'" Business Insider, August 19, 2016. www.businessinsider.my.
43. Quoted in Elizabeth Kolbert, "Our Automated Future," *New Yorker*, December 19, 2016. www.newyorker.com.
44. Quoted in Siddhartha Mukherjee, "A.I. Versus M.D.," *New Yorker*, April 3, 2017. www.newyorker.com.

45. Quoted in Will Knight, "Could AI Solve the World's Biggest Problems?," *MIT Technology Review*, January 12, 2016. www.technologyreview.com.

46. Quoted in Knight, "Could AI Solve the World's Biggest Problems?"

47. Ben Goertzel, "AI Will Surpass Human Ability Before the Century Is Over," Big Think, February 5, 2017. http://bigthink .com.

48. Goertzel, "AI Will Surpass Human Ability Before the Century Is Over."

49. Quoted in Samuel Gibbs, "Elon Musk: Artificial Intelligence Is Our Biggest Existential Threat," *Guardian* (Manchester), October 27, 2014. www.theguardian.com.

50. Quoted in Rory Cellan-Jones, "Stephen Hawking Warns Artificial Intelligence Could End Mankind," BBC, December 2, 2014. www.bbc.com.

51. Quoted in Michael Rundle, "Artificial Intelligence Warning Says Research Must Avoid Apocalyptic 'Pitfalls,'" *Huffington Post* (UK), December 1, 2015. www.huffingtonpost.co.uk.

52. Nick Bostrom, "What Happens When Our Computers Get Smarter Than We Are?," TED, March 2015. www.ted.com.

53. Neil deGrasse Tyson, Twitter, August 8, 2014. https://twitter .com.

CHAPTER 4
SOLUTIONS: Combine Human and Artificial Intelligence

54. Quoted in Tim Urban, "Neuralink and the Brain's Magical Future," *Wait but Why* (blog), April 20, 2017. http://waitbutwhy .com.

55. Kelly Clancy, "A Computer to Rival the Brain," *New Yorker*, February 15, 2017. www.newyorker.com.

56. Jim Guszcza et al., "Cognitive Collaboration," Deloitte University Press, January 23, 2017. https://dupress.deloitte.com.

57. Maurice Conti, "The Incredible Inventions of Intuitive AI," TED, February 2017. www.ted.com.

58. Conti, "The Incredible Inventions of Intuitive AI."

59. Quoted in Amy Ellis Nutt, "In a Medical First, Brain Implant Allows Paralyzed Man to Feel Again," *Washington Post*, October 13, 2016. www.washingtonpost.com.
60. Quoted in Nutt, "In a Medical First, Brain Implant Allows Paralyzed Man to Feel Again."
61. Peter Diamandis, "The Brain Tech to Merge Humans and AI Is Already Being Developed," Singularity Hub, December 5, 2016. https://singularityhub.com.
62. Ray Kurzweil, "Get Ready for Hybrid Thinking," TED, March 2014. www.ted.com.
63. Quoted in Urban, "Neuralink and the Brain's Magical Future."
64. Urban, "Neuralink and the Brain's Magical Future."
65. Urban, "Neuralink and the Brain's Magical Future."
66. Kurzweil, "Get Ready for Hybrid Thinking."
67. Shelly Fan, "New Artificial Synapse Bridges the Gap to Brain-Like Computers," Singularity Hub, March 15, 2017. https://singularityhub.com.
68. Quoted in Fan, "New Artificial Synapse Bridges the Gap to Brain-Like Computers."
69. Quoted in Fan, "New Artificial Synapse Bridges the Gap to Brain-Like Computers."

FIND OUT MORE

Books
Nick Bostrom, *Superintelligence: Paths, Dangers, Strategies.* Oxford: Oxford University Press, 2016.

Brian Christian and Tom Griffiths, *Algorithms to Live By: The Computer Science of Human Decisions.* New York: Holt, 2016.

Pedro Domingos, *The Master Algorithm: How the Quest for the Ultimate Learning Machine Will Remake Our World.* New York: Perseus, 2015.

Luke Dormehl, *Thinking Machines: The Quest for Artificial Intelligence.* New York: Penguin, 2017.

Michio Kaku, *The Future of the Mind: The Scientific Quest to Understand, Enhance, and Empower the Mind.* New York: Anchor, 2015.

Seong-Whan Lee, Heinrich H. Bulthoff, and Klaus-Robert Muller, eds., *Recent Progress in Brain and Cognitive Engineering*. New York: Springer, 2015.

Internet Sources
Robert Epstein, "The Empty Brain," *Aeon*, May 18, 2016. https://aeon.co/essays/your-brain-does-not-process-information-and-it-is-not-a-computer.

Will Knight, "The Dark Secret at the Heart of AI," *MIT Technology Review*, April 11, 2017. www.technologyreview.com/s/604087/the-dark-secret-at-the-heart-of-ai.

Christof Koch, "How the Computer Beat the Go Master," *Scientific American*, March 19, 2016. www.scientificamerican.com/article/how-the-computer-beat-the-go-master.

Gideon Lewis-Kraus, "The Great A.I. Awakening," *New York Times*, December 14, 2016. www.nytimes.com/2016/12/14/magazine/the-great-ai-awakening.html.

Emily Singer, "Mapping the Brain to Build Better Machines," *Quanta Magazine*, April 6, 2016. www.quantamagazine.org/20160406-brain-maps-micron-program-iarpa.

Stanford University, "One Hundred Year Study on Artificial Intelligence," September 2016. https://ai100.stanford.edu/2016-report.

Tim Urban, "The AI Revolution: The Road to Superintelligence," *Wait but Why* (blog), January 22, 2015. http://waitbutwhy.com/2015/01/artificial-intelligence-revolution-1.html.

Tim Urban, "Neuralink and the Brain's Magical Future," *Wait but Why* (blog), April 20, 2017. http://waitbutwhy.com/2017/04/neuralink.html.

Websites

Singularity Hub (https://singularityhub.com). Singularity Hub publishes articles on technological progress and scientific breakthroughs aimed at the lay reader. It contains hundreds of articles on the newest breakthroughs in artificial intelligence and the brain.

TED (www.ted.com). TED (Technology, Entertainment, Design) conferences bring together experts to share ideas in the form of short presentations. Its website contains over two thousand of these presentations, including hundreds on topics like the brain, neuroscience, artificial intelligence, machine learning, and robotics.

INDEX

75

PICTURE CREDITS

ABOUT THE AUTHOR

Christine Wilcox writes fiction and nonfiction for young adults and adults. She has worked as an editor, an instructional designer, and a writing instructor. She lives in Richmond, Virginia, with her husband, David, and her son, Doug.